FRESH OCEANS

●

an anthology of poetry
by Scottish women

146004/891·6313

Scottish women's publisher

Published by STRAMULLION Limited 1989
11a Forth Street, Edinburgh EH1 3LE

British Library Cataloguing in Publication Data

Fresh oceans: an anthology of poetry by Scottish women.
  1. Poetry in English. Scottish writers, to 1988 – Anthologies
  2. Poetry in Scottish Gaelic, 1930 –. English Texts.
  821'.008'099411
  891.6'313

  ISBN 0-907343-09-0

Acknowledgements

The following poems have previously been published elsewhere:

'An déidh an tòrraidh/After the funeral' in *Chapman*; 'Gangrel's Sang' in *Nor East Neuk* (Rainbow Enterprises); 'What is written' in *Cencrastus*; 'A terrain' in *Writing Women*; 'Wumman movan' in *Lines Review*; 'Clearances' and 'Peter the Rock' in *The Way We Live* (Bloodaxe); 'A woman alone' in *Chapman*; 'full circle' in *Graffiti*; 'A woman's muse' in *Chapman*; 'Chambered cairn' in *Lines Review*; 'Silk moth ghosts' in *New Writing Scotland 1984*.

The publisher acknowledges subsidy from the Scottish Arts Council towards the publicaton of this volume.

Front cover design: Anna Ingleby

Typeset and printed by Polyprint
48 Pleasance, Edinburgh EH8 9TJ

Contents

Publisher's preface

Stramullion's first publication, *Hens in the Hay*, was a collection of poetry coming from a writers' workshop based in Edinburgh. It was received enthusiastically by both the press and public. We realised that this book showed only a fraction of the kind of poetry which is being written by women all over Scotland, and so we decided to publish a much broader anthology which would show something of the range and diversity of women's poetry in the 'eighties.

The result is *Fresh Oceans* – by no means a definitive or all-inclusive anthology, and very much a personal selection by members of Stramullion. We hope it will lead you to explore more of the wealth of women's poetry in Scotland. We've enjoyed putting this book together and hope you will enjoy reading it.

Introduction

The Scottish Poetry Library put on an exhibition in January 1986 of work by Scottish women poets, and the resulting catalogue listed as many as forty-five. This included women of earlier times as well as women writing today – many of whom were published in literary magazines or writers' workshop anthologies, but less than half of whom had been published in book form. Comparatively speaking, most of them were 'unknown'. Indeed the average member of the Scottish literati would probably not have heard of more than two or three; and students would have great difficulty in finding interviews, critical material, sound or video recordings on which to base a study. This anthology is therefore a mere selection, but, along with other recent anthologies and recordings, important not so much for the gap as for the huge chasm it is helping to fill.

It is apparent that specifically womens' publishing has helped to bring women poets more into public awareness. For a long time there have been women composing and publishing poetry, particularly in Gaeldom and the North East of Scotland, but they seemed somehow not to count, or to be counted. For every one who produced an occasional book of poems there must have been twenty or fifty who wrote and never told, or certainly never presumed to take their own work seriously. The reticence traditionally required of women – keeping to the private rather than the public sphere – together with a more general Scottish reticence, perhaps acted as a repressant on women letting their voices be heard through poetry. It may be no coincidence that poets such as Christina Rossetti, Emily Dickinson, Hilda Doolittle, Stevie Smith, and perhaps our own Helen Cruikshank, have had to live life very much alone, facing a lack of understanding and encouragement of the right kind.

It can be argued that it is not in women's best interests to be grouped together as women poets, but that they should be regarded as poets, each with her own voice and style, in the same way as other poets. Poetry is as varied in form, content, style and mode as music is, or art. Women too, come in infinite varieties, and a particular woman writer may have more in common with another poet who may be male, but shares more of her background and experience, than other women writers as such. The shared background for all the women in this book is, of course, living in Scotland today.

Poetry has been classified in our century in the popular mind as something studied at university and practised by literary men. It has tended not to be considered among the practising· contemporary arts, taking its place alongside music, drama, dance and painting. The lack of provision for students and apprentice poets bears out this state of affairs. Writing poetry, or admitting to it, is very often still a matter of embarrassment and apology, certainly until one is retired or dead. The status accorded to the 'poet' in our society has traditionally been a high one – one too high to be given any monetary value – and by implication too high for the majority of men and all women. Whereas women have become great opera singers because opera needs women's voices, poetry has not seemed to need women's voices.

During the '80s, women writers have been meeting one another, discussing their situation and accepting a serious commitment to their metier. But dedication to anything as personal as writing poetry is often regarded as selfish and unnatural in women; or they are termed neurotic and 'hysterical' (a word which technically means womanly). With the woman poet it could be suggested that, in Jungian terms, it is her animus that writes out of the matrix of the feminine, whereas in men poets it is the anima (the muse) that writes out of the matrix of the masculine. This is the reversal that seems to demand a rethinking and redefining of criteria.

This anthology shows experimentation and fluidity, an exploratory mode, based on the extreme boldness and 'selfishness' of daring to explore oneself – how it really is to be a women of today's world, how it feels, what matters, what doesn't matter, how she interacts with people, ideas and circumstances to become an integrated, articulate artist in words, however limited or constrained in lifestyle.

The overall impression from this anthology is that these particular women poets are exulting in the practice of their art. They enjoy using words to explore what is happening to and within them now, not, as Eliot said is so often the case, 'for the thing one no longer has to say'. Even where there is distress or sorrow in the subject matter the poems are life-affirming and life-creating, not in any naive or simplistic way, but in a wisely innocent way.

This is an anthology to enjoy, to become immersed in, and to share with others. These women poets are, in Chris Cherry's words, 'testing the limits', but not in order to draw back, rather to go over them and break new ground.

Tessa Ransford
Director, The Scottish Poetry Library

Because

Because we painted your bedroom together, and then you fell sick
with the smell of the paint, the party was cancelled.
That was the summer it rained at the cottage. I taught you to sew.
You made a pink traycloth to give to your aunt; segments
of communal life strung, beadlike, on a communal string. So
with the ondrift of time, either the beads get eroded
from all that nestling and bumping together or
the thread stretches, wears thin and it snaps and
beads fall in irretrievable scatter and clatter
and this time it can't be restrung; I never
counted them, I can't be sure of finding them all.
They no longer belong to me anyway, but to
the dust under the piano, the crack
in the skirting, the bowl of pot-pourri,
its five-year-old roses barely disturbed.
I cannot thole them without the gradation
of consequence, making no sense on their own,
still bearing the imprint of precedence lost.
The cat finds something, and teaches her kittens a game.
I let her. They seem to have made their choice. But
the clasps lodge under my nails, small strings hang from my hands.

Kate Armstrong

An déidh an tòrraidh

Tha a' bhanntrach na seasamh aig an doras
a ceann an taic a' bhalla.
Tha gach rud sàmhach.
Tha na h-aoighean air am biadhadh
is a' mhòr-chuid air falbh,
am bàgh 's am baile glas glas,
's na bàtaichean-iasgaich a'cur a-mach gun fhuaim.
Cluinnidh i còmhradh nam bana-chàirdean sa' chidsin
is na bodaich, len dramannan,
a'bruidhinn air beatha dheagh-bheusach.
"Ann an doigh 's e latha toilichte a bh'againn"
tha i ag ràdh, a'coimhead a mic,
is aogas an athar
ann an aodann gach fir dhiubh.

Gu h-obann sàthaidh a' ghrian a-mach bannan
soluis liomaid-bhuidhe
thar nan raon de dh'fhochann gruamach,
is sguabar suip de cheò airgid
an àirde 's air falbh
thar a' bhàigh agus briosgaidh na clèibh
gaol an fhir mhairbh dhan t-saoghal,
is tionndaidh i a-steach
le deòirean na sùilean.

Meg Bateman

2

After the funeral

The widow stands at the door
and leans her hand against the wall.
All is quiet.
The guests are fed
and mostly gone,
and the sea and the town are grey, grey,
with the fishing boats silently putting out.
She hears the talk of the women in the kitchen
and the old men with their drams
discussing a life well-lived.
"It's kind of been a happy day"
she says, looking at her boys,
each with his father's
likeness in his face.

Suddenly the sun stabs out bars
of lemon-yellow light
over the fields of glowering corn,
and wisps of mist
are whisked up and away
over the sea and she quickens
with the dead man's love for the world,
and turns back into the house
with tears in her eyes.

Meg Bateman

Rut san ospadal

Cearcall air chearcall
nì do chorrag air mo bhriogais —
saoghalan nach fhaic mi,
ceòl nach cluinn mi . . .

Beag air bheag
tha an cloc aig a' bhalla
a'sreap ris an uair.
Cuiridh mi do làmh far mo ghlùine.
"S fheàrr dhomh falbh."
is tha do chorp nam ghàirdeanan
mar liùdhaig.

Boireannach trom aosda
a'tarraing gun fhios tro na sràidean dorcha
geumnaich bho bhuailtean an taigh-spadaidh,
fulangas 's fèitheamh;
och am feitheamh 's am fulangas,
och thusa, thusa,

maith dhuinn, a Dhia.

Meg Bateman

4

Ruth in hospital

Round and round
goes your finger on my trousers –
worlds I can't see,
music I can't hear . . .

Little by little
the clock on the wall
struggles towards the hour.
I set your hand from my knee.
"I'd better go."
and your body in my arms
is like a rag-doll.

An old heavy woman
shuffling unnoticed through the streets,
lowing from the slaughter-house pens,
suffering and waiting;
oh, the waiting and the suffering,
oh you, you,

God, forgive us.

Meg Bateman

Dealbh mo mhàthar

Bha mo mhàthair ag innse dhomh
gun tig eilid gach feasgar
a-mach às a'choille dhan achadh fhèoir,
an aon tè, 's dòcha,
a dh'àraich iad an-uiridh,
is i a'tilleadh a-nist le a h-àl.

Chan e gràs an fhèidh fhìnealta
a' glusad thar na leargainn
a leanas ri m'inntinn, na fos
a dà mheann, crùibte còmhla,
ach aodann mo mhàthar 's i a'bruidhinn,
is a guth, cho toilicht, cho blàth.

Picture of my mother

My mother was telling me
that a hind comes every evening
out of the wood into the hay-field,
the same one probably
they fed last year,
returning now with her young.

It isn't the grace of the doe
moving across the slope
that lingers in my mind, nor yet
the two fawns huddled together,
but my mother's face as she spoke,
and her voice, so excited, so warm.

Meg Bateman

6

Palette

Reid.
Hips an haws,
Hairt's bluid.
Blue.
The fairy hue,
Forget-me-not,
Rue.
Yalla.
Coordy,
Gowden,
Gay,
Breem spray.
Green.
Girsse,
Greivin, hearse;
Weirin green,
Ye's weir black afore its deen.
Broon.
Moosie's goun,
Peat-burn
Whummlin doon.
Black.
Sorra,
Gomorrah.
Purple.
Thistle, heather, thyme
Thon's mine.

Sheena Blackhall

girsse: grass   whummlin: overturning

7

Dawn an Gloam

She steers, half-drooned in sleep,
Druggit wi dwaumin
Dreams link hauns an flee, nicht-thistledown
Blawn, b' the lip o waukfulness.
She's roused, and raxxin. Shaddow-thocts
Wither an flee, like frichtit fawns.
Her ootflung airm's wids strauchenin.
Her bare flank's widlan roses,
Blinkin ben the sheuch.
Blearie wabs o gossamer, her eyelids,
Shak their midnicht spiders,
Scuttlin till the neuk.
The snell win weets her broo.
Aathing's new
The cairryin cries o birds
Rise till the reidenin sun
Her in-drawn braith's
The rise an drap o oceans.
In her wame, the black lan meeves.
Ower her sma breists, the clouds weave lichtly
The green an pleasant dawn.

The gloam's a cailleach,
Dodderin ben the mirk
A hyterin fitfa, far the corbies caw,
Ferfochen, trauchelt, blae.
Skin-thin o bluid.
Till Nicht, wi infinite peety
Rowes her droopin heid
In a black shawl. Gloam sighs,
Her sap ootrun, blinks aff her tears
Her greetin's hyne abeen
The glintin starnies,
Set abeen the meen
As sinkin doon, the gloamin,
Gently meets the grun.

Gangrel's sang

At nicht fin the bairns are bedded doon
The hash o the day set by
I climm the stairs, as a wife maun dee
An lie, far a wife maun lie.

Twa sleepers, close as braith itsel
Rowed in the linen fine
His een shut, peacefu, calm, and quate
The restless dark in mine

Fain wid I slip till a braid, braid muir
Wi the wins that hae nae hame
Rin wi the stag, an the secret deer
Far the settin sun's a flame

Nae mist sae thick, bit love can pierce't
An the cry o the geese rings free
Hearth an hoose are his hale delicht
It's the open road, that beckons me.

Bound an wound b' a band o gowd
Twined-bit jined in nocht.
He raxxes oot tae touch a wife –
I turn, tae haud a thocht.

Sheena Blackhall

dwaumin: day-dreaming
sheuch: ditch
neuk: corner
cailleach: old woman
ferfochen: exhausted
blae: lead-coloured
raxxin: stretching
snell: sharp, piercing

meeves: moves
corbies: ravens
trauchelt: work-wearied

gangrel: vagrant
gowd: gold
hash: noisy tumult
raxxes: stretches

9

Chernobyl – St. Abbs, May 1986

Did you have rain on your tongue
As you laughed that day
And a wind soft at your cheek
To tell you of the weather that would come?

Did you have lichen growing
Yellow on red rocks
Water to splash at your ankles
A beach of sand
Grains to your flesh clinging ?

Did you have milk on your lip
As you put the cup down
Gasped from the long swig
You took halfway through
That hot morning ?

Was there a stalk to chew
A leaf to munch
Down in the depths of the warm grasses
A berry to stain your lips with red?

And the warm spring
Suddenly there
Touch of kind air
And birds flying through
The blue layers
Of what is sometimes called
Heaven; did you have this
To tell you of the clear
State of the future
The possible dream
Your own way, your one life
Growing through you like grass
Thick with insects, wet with dew?

Did you have
Mornings like this
With no reason to shut the doors?

And now do you want the time back
And the air back
Transparent as truth
And the clear rain
Falling again like tears
And no harm done?

The wind blows small clouds
In from the east.
I come out of doors
The sea's breath sharpens
There is glitter on the rocks
White in the waves
The sun touches me
There is water in the leaves.
I think of you, a child
With milk upon your lip
Believing as I have to
In the clean air
The new morning.

II

The words are the ones we trusted
All of us: grass, milk, rain,
Leaf.
There was bloom on the fruit
The effortless sheen on skin.
There was growing
From childhood to old age
There was truth.

Where shall we turn now
For a clear bite
For a deep breath
For daring to live?
Where shall we live
And in what, if these things
Be ashes, lies?

What shall we swim in
How shall we dream
And how feed
Not only the numberless new
Mouths of need
But that deep ache
For what renews, renews, renews?

Rosalind Brackenbury

Flying to Ireland/Lying on the sofa with Keiran

Flying low enough to see
Waves wrinkle at shore-lines
Mountains flatten as bodies do
That lie at rest; you come
Close to the earth.
It is the detail of beauty
That fascinates
I can never have enough of looking

Flying this low
Coming up this close
Skimming all at once the coast of Ireland
Lifted above the sea
You are looking at me as if
I too were this earth
These two coastlines
These hills scored white with snow
And small green fields at last
Where horses stand stock still

Flying this low above me
One hand outstretched
You come to rest; we tip
Closer to earth, swing
To the bright globe
Come down from thinner air
To a landing peace
A gentle bump, a sigh
And, minutes before me,
You sleep.

Rosalind Brackenbury

We were discussing . . .

We were discussing such huge questions
and eventually I felt so tired that¯
if there had been a little stone jug
of maybe terracotta with blue painted flowers
on the side or
handle I would have poured the contents
over my cheek and brow not caring
if it was milk or water
because milk would have meant the
musky homeliness of the grazing cow and
water the lucid reflecting lake
beside which we were lying
and talking

Sunset in a wild place

As I passed your sky
I saw that it was burning.
Did you know?

My watching eye travelled up
To the place where
The bleak tree lances

The heavens and as you see
By my red coat sleeve
The rain turned to blood.

Sarah Busbridge

14

Afternoon succulence

Gaze over uncut orange
heated summer garden's
hard dull haze
marble silence

knife to segment
heated orange hard
garden gaze
summer marble

dull squeezed haze
silent summer segment
hard marble garden

Statue

Sarah Busbridge

Blood flower

Blood flower
voluptuously licks
arcs of flame
across black vellum.

Lapped in warm influence
trembling current
floats down liquid curves,
gold lustred slide.

Ebony corona buffed to sheen
ante-room charged with golden light
hovering bee daring to risk
honey mine.

Gold light poured into a golden cup.

Chris Cherry

Testing the limits

The cage door opened
and a bird fell through

rested her weight against the singing drift
and flew.

Before this we had felt in the dark
along a wall, fumbled
for a door, a key, a keyhole
the light apparent only around the shadows
our eyes unaccustomed, not knowing
what we would find there

as if standing before death
waiting for the poem that says it all
for more than the crude manifestation
of an inner vision, waiting
for what was not yet visible.

Does the earth ache, waiting
for the time to put forth flowers?
Does the sea wait for the tide to turn?

I do not speak of a dream

a fantasy of new leaves floating
against a botomless sky

I speak of root and trunk and branches
of sap and stem
changed and renewed in time.

I speak of you and me
testing the limits of desire.

Chris Cherry

The Tooth Fairy

I am
The Tooth Fairy
     Doubling as Santa Claws.
Just lose a tooth
     Lose a tooth? How careless can you get?
And I'll be there
Any day of the year
     Days?
     Since when did I get to work days?
I work while you sleep
But I never sleep
I fly over the world
To watch children lose teeth.
     Stupid thing to reward.
Overtime? What's that?
     Double nothing is nothing.
Join a union? Why?
     They wouldn't take me.
But sometimes – I'm sorry –
I forget the way
     Get drunk
Or didn't notice a toothipeg
Till the next day
     Someone didn't tell their mum?
     Why apologise anyway?

     I am the Tooth and Claws Fairy
     I travel round subverting little girls
     persuading them their best friends are each other
     and Christmas is a lie about a father
     (or else that Mary was a surrogate mother)
     and losing teeth is just a bloody nuisance . . .
     and speaking of a bloody nuisance –
     you know what I mean, the real bloody nuisance –
     why isn't that provided with a fairy ?

Maggie Christie

Persian tapestry

I sit on woven mosses
tongue of leopard
tasting my feet,
the whip of its master
cutting my thigh.
I am warmed by the
dampened wood, cut
from the orchard
which embraces
the lawn.
I watch from the floor
the air mottled like
marble, streaks of
grey and black,
and he tells me
the moon shines
because the sun
reflects her like a
piece of glass.
I struggle to stand
careful of the
carpet twine,
I open the window
and feel the night air
rush at me, waves to a
blind man, and I see
the ancient smoothed
ivory moon and know
her smile is not
because of him.

Barbara Clarke

El Norte

The skull flesh seems soft as velvet
embalming brains in life and death,
but loose enough to secure a hook
which pierces through, holding a rope
which holds the head; bodiless.
They shut his eyes, the lashes dark
enough to make shadows which, like
tears trail down his stiff cheeks
and his mouth cocked open as if he
waits to drink from ice fountains.
He is suspended from one of few trees
still alive, the bark ashen and crawling
with lice, gaping hollows.
Beneath, the purpling sand, skeletal
remnants.

Barbara Clarke

Chile 1974

With one hand he twirls his pistol,
in the other takes his cup
and drinks. Every Sunday it
is wine turned into blood
and he falls drunk in the street
where the afternoon shadows
lurch at him, sinister and grey
and crawl behind him until he is home.

In his room he washes off the blood
and ties his clothes
in rubbish bags.
He splashes on his perfume
waits for Consuela.
She comes eventually
bringing flowers and cake
and laughing, stretches out her arms,
pulling to her all man's failing.

In the church a statue,
a halo of stars welded
by the blacksmith
and she holds out her arms
wantonly.

Barbara Clarke

A rescued lamb

The smell of wet tweed is near rancid.
Sharp and close, the wool tickles my nose.
I'm slung in rough folds round a broad back.
The world smells only of my mother, cold.

Rocking, walking,
looking at the thick neck of my carrier,
hearing his boots on wet moorland,
I am trapped, resigned
and disappear inside myself to pass the time.

The boots hit the hard earth of the track,
then cobbles of a yard.
I feel my sling shift from its moorings
and for the second time I am born.

Tipped out onto cold stone,
I teeter to my feet and feel the spaces
between each leg and under my belly,
the thin, open air.

My bleat for help almost topples me over.
When a teat is offered
it has no muzzling comfort:
cold sustenance I suck dry.

The cool blue air in my nostrils separates each smell.
I find the grey stone walls by moss and dampness.
The barn steams warm with straw, golden and heady.
The sharp green field sends soft breaths of creamy clover.

Each scent flows distinct
as each free leg I stand on.
Never again will the world
smell heavy of mother.

Dot Clarke

Travel tales

1   Lift Off

Such a flat life I lead –
an airport runway
lying in long stretches
of grey and green,
going nowhere.

Until a decision to leave
gathers friends and family
to waft me fromteh flat life
into a lift off
on layers of love.

2   Landings

Drop me somewhere new
and I duck behind parapets
to crouch, tense and wary.

I listen to new languages
and slowly peer over my stone wall
at new surroundings.

After watching, waiting,
and smiling a lot,
I try my own stumbling phrases.

If greeted with a smile,
more of me will emerge
until I hop up to perch on warm stone.

In the glow of sunset, I flex my wings
and soar on my own song
to new landings.

3   Homecoming

The hardest part
about coming home
is telling the tales.

As we hugged hello
the thing itself stopped.
All that was left
was to account for the time.

I try to describe the difference,
spin yarns from here
to there and back again.

But all I can do
is smile silently
and blink with a brighter eye.

Dot Clarke

Hans and Deiter, February 1985

My kitchen is full of Germans.
I used to dream
Bad men were after me.
They were always Germans.

We were in the dark
Because of the Germans.
There was no chocolate
Because of the Germans.
"Look, Mummy, I've squashed
This worm. It was a German."

Now Hans and Deiter stand over
My little fair-haired daughter.
She says, "Deiter, can you read
This book to me?
It's German."

Now my kitchen (two floors up)
Becomes the forest hut.
Beyond patchwork curtains
Wolves howl for miles.
The kindly woodcutter
Takes the child upon his knee.
The door opens and in comes
The enchanted bear:
"Snow white, Rose red
Would you have your sweetheart dead?"
Dead in Dresden, dead in Belsen.
My little girl doesn't know
These names.

Who's coming out of the forest
To swallow her ?

Helen Dunwoodie

25

Garden in New England, looking homeward

"You'll know".
My mind clears: another garden speaks to me;
Soil I recognise.
Crops swell: peas, onions, carrots, scarlet runner beans,
I name as kin to other seeds I sowed.
This ring of herbs weaves its familiar spell,
Pungent and sharp, a pang beneath my ribs;
And strangers green in welcome, quietly burgeoning.
I know them: zucchini, tomato, pepper, pumpkin,
Melon and squash.
Earth warms to my bare feet:
"You'll know".
Sweet compost, piled leaves of careful years –
A husbandry so like my own
I am at peace here.
A gardner is never a stranger
Wherever the earth is wooed and brought to bear.
So great a gift is mine:
"You'll know".

I know.
So thank the earth for all such gifts,
I know.
No I am not born to suffer,
But to recognise;
Not to hurt nor be hurt,
Only to comprehend;
Not to seek fulfilment,
But to have it shower sudden upon me
In the quiet evening, surprising my eyes
That strained to catch some illusion farther off.

I have a garden over the sea,
My green Eden,
Where apples thicken from withered buds,
Soft fruit ripens purple and red
Tanging the earth with berry scents.
White roses lean across my window.
A tiger lily opens
Exotic among poppies and the phlox.
Oh my camellia, sweet pea, myrtle and lavender,
If I had never known you,
You would accomplish no such garden there.

I recall you all, intrepid travellers,
Voyaging here in my mind's eye.
You are the seeds within my core;
Yes I am at home in gardens.
I know.

Margaret Elphinstone

Island

And how the land cries out to me:
The lowness of it, a strip
Suspended betweeen air and water,
Earth precious as emerald;
Rainwashed, sheepshaven,
Sheer shores inviting me
To be responsible for my own death.

Life is a choice
Wrung out of a thin soil,
Wrested from an indifferent sea.
I watched waves tower against red cliffs
And the breaking of them
Shook my body, pressed against the thrift.
The island has been mine.
I have taken seisin
Rightfully. My lamp burned
Across the water, and by my presence
the boats were guided home.

Margaret Elphinstone

To my friend who is a woman and a poet, like me

You called me a poet
and took me in your arms, laughing
with the terror of it. So close –
And I, shut down, dreaming of a stranger
shedding his sealskin while the moon rose
over an empty beach – I did not see you,
though I looked into the black pits
of your eyes, and held you
breasts against breasts, your image
mine, and I, the same as you.

You called me a poet.
You – the poet –
So now I will believe you
I will take your gift and make words of it;
Perhaps I am falling
into another love, that expects nothing.
You kissed me – you –
but no man ever said I was a poet.

I wish you a lover, gentle as the waves on the beach
that is perhaps less empty when we are not there.
I wish you the invisible dance
on the shores of consciousness,
slipping back to the sea at daylight.
I wish you poetry
and lust, kisses deep and salt as the sea,
words that pierce like morning,
love poured down, running over the sand into water.
And because you say I am a poet,
I wish myself the same.

Margaret Elphinstone

Death Cap

The work of man
on the forest floor:
light let in, lopped trees.
The work of nature:
mysteries.
The work of children:
sticks for games,
feathers for pleasure,
fircones, acorns.
The work of squirrels;
broken bark.
The work of a fox:
scattered bones.

A mixed wood.
Mushrooms fling up,
ominous, unreal
Death cap, grey
or horrid green.

A woman, I walk
in the wood.
I know the Death Cap
is bad, I know it without books,
it is creepy,
I beware,
I treat it
with proper fear.
Children, I lead you
acorns in your pockets
to the wood's perimeter
and future sun.

Sally Evans

What is written

What is written is the stating of absence
of the failure of glory to intervene
in the scraping blueness
on slaty light-deflecting roofs

The inability of light to distribute vision
or to pinpoint in the hazy drumming of a car
the recognizable exterior of another life
Its inability to clarify a man on a roof
or the lemon opaqueness of a plastic sack
to signify something of the present
in a mundane activity
a certain absorption in the sun and warmth
a certain allowing of the days to be the days

(even in August   month of repossession
by acute and devouring futures)

It does not follow that the days constitute stillness

The hours are restlessly transfixed and move
I am compacted and dispersed by the blades

What is written bears witness
to the heedless calamity of its own inexistence

                         to its minute destruction
in a shaky kitchen where the peeled onion skins
the emptied milk cartons
are a disordering flood-tide

What is written bears witness to murder
in the language of the victim
to a mundane and daily absence

What is written bears witness to a woman drowning

Gerrie Fellows

A terrain

I find myself in a landscape
which cannot be worked
A terrain of metal and too much ash
A soil in which inert things pause
precluding lushness

Here I can grow nothing
but a few hasty traveller's plants
Or line a rucksack with dried herbs

Storm damage forbids the garden

In each place I bivouac
build hurried shelter

What compass has driven me into this country
to become a tent dweller
Exile from the earth of the slow root
knowing how to move fast among the cities

Where I pitch my tent are bones
the charred remains of fire
I cannot wait and grow old
watching for the green fronds.

I am looking for a river valley
on a map from which the signs
of orchards   planted fields
have been erased   Rain
and my own recurring thumbprint
have left merely the faint bedrock

A sign spells brackish water

But no community of nomads arrives
to plant here a green-leafed food
build walls against the north-east wind
weave blankets in which to wrap a child

On this terrain there is no means

The cartographers cannot indicate
the places of cultivation
Worn thin like folded silk
and stiff with candlewax
the maps have become a history
record of a falling into
bleak territories in the mind
where minutiae of spiralling forms
a tender growth
                    remain unmarked
unsignified

What is mapped becomes the known

Outside the scope of its contours
flattened signs
hankering roots reach
deep into an essential chemistry
of water

Gerrie Fellows

33

Haarsang

wan wyle nicht o haar
ye sang
my sang
fardaraar.

nou
wha cud iver
thoull
a sang

wi the warl
aa
fullo
haar ?

Carol Galbraith

Wumman movan

Fae the hert o the warl's lowe
I wacht ye
greetan
in a hotchan howe.

I socht tae catch ye
but Grief wheept alang
shoran the rush-hour thrang.

Whitwye haes Memry fun ye
hauf a lifespan dune
loupan owre the locusts in their beerial grunn

tae grup thon lang-forgotten pain
that lowet aroon your sair-begrotten face
lowsan the haps o age an space.

Sweel seen the burd ye war
haes braith int yet
tae gar
ye cowp stravaigin starns

an scliffer aa owre Mars
an mouger thru the centre air
aye warsslan
intae the hert o the warl's sun.

Carol Galbraith

Anno-wreck-sick

I am Anorexic   I mean
I really think thin   real lean   I
mean   I've been carried away to
the point where I've all but
disappeared.

Poor virgin, poor maiden, I was – oh
they wanted me fed up plump, firm, fair, oh
so femininely fattened for the
rutting rites – they wanted me sweet flesh to be
some sacrifice on the altar bed of adulthood.

Anno Wreck Sick – I could
play around with the hollow sound of it
play frantic antics with semantics   but
that's not what you want to know   oh no let's
get right down to the nitty, dig to the dying bone
search in my shrinking skull the meaty matter of it.

So you want to know why I don't
want to grow oh please think of what it –
sweet sixteen get preened for prodding, fumbling
grunting, mumbling while small child me inside
dies crumbling.

Scars will heal
Shrink and heal
Shrink my head
I want to be dead.

Cut off your bloody nose, my ma
always said, to spite, she said,
oh ma, how right, how right.

Please don't pin my body, man
lovely living butterfly, please
don't try   I'd sooner die.

So I'll waste the flesh away, ruin
your chances, forestall your advances.

Anorexic, that's what I am,
happy to be carried away with
a rattling laugh in my skinny throat
to my sweet deathbed.

Magi Gibson

In a Galloway wood

By the alley of limes
                along the way
crowd ancient tombstones
                    carved angel heads.
Moss and mildew
            eat away the words.

Barred ruined transept
              of the roofless chapel
named for the knights,
                St.John of Jerusalem:
here kings and queens came
              to cross at the ford.

A great grey-green stone
               in a Galloway wood
with the hollow pool
             quite perfect
filled with rainwater
             and red rowan-berries:

a holy water basin
            on the border of the walk.
"Keep away", the minister
               warned his villagers,
"in this a lost child
           lay and drowned."

But the sun suddenly
              shining on shadows
hollow and throaty
             sound the hooves
fording by the old way
             paved under the water.

And the sun works
        as the snow does
on a wisp of green corn
        in workaday clothes,
in sweatshirt, shorts
        and muddy sandals,

a little lass
        laughs near the stone
with her crown
        of tawny hair,
an incarnation
        of the pilgrims' way.

Sunlight clothes her
        in a timeless space,
endows a Galloway wood
        with a new Devorgilla,
a young sweetheart
        again for Scotland.

Valerie Gillies

(Devorgilla: Devorguilla, 13th century lady of Galloway)

Unspoken words of a North Uist woman, 1901

Ach. It's one of them again gesturing at me
as if I were cattle and he the cowman.
His face is too pale and unlined for that
and his walk too slow and aimless.
They are forgetful people
these 'camera' men.
They make a picture
with that box to look at
in their southern houses
so they can remember.
As if it mattered to them.

If it mattered to them
they would remember the smell of the machair
the slick ousha of the peat from the tuskar
the pull of a full creel of the peats.
And the feet peat-grimed, swollen from the cold
and too much walking.
The ceaseless click, click, click of the needles
as we walk with our creels and talk with our mouths
each task a little lighter if another can be done with it.
They have no task to do
but to point and gesture and prod
as if we were cattle, dumb, forgetful
lost in our tracks.

I mind it all, no 'camera', but I mind.
The sting of the peat water
when I bathed for my wedding.
I mind the waiting for the calving
and the bull calf dead, useless.
The body wearing Alisdair's jersey with my stitches:
the twisted blackberry and the wandering wave.
And I mind the leg that never healed
after the ram kicked when I clipped him
the first time.
I mind so much, my face is lined
with the hurt of it.
If having a 'camera' means you can forget
there is some use for it here.

Thelma Good

Miss Currer Bell

Your wren frame
and rib cage
(brittle as the picked bones
of a baked capon)

trod slimy flagstones
in flimsy shoes
where you shivered
in churches, expiating
not *your* sin but
the cant of others.

You saw them all die,
including the profligate
brother

from consumption, bad water
and cold kitchen floors:
Ellis, with her heath-wanderings
and intractable will and
Acton, docile and willing
to give herself to her Maker.

Your fame never cooled
your rage,
but in a snowdrop dress
you gave yourself to a
clod whose possession
killed you.

Mary Gladstone

Cat in labour

Round bellied
she sang
and slunk,
moaning
low and heavy
groundwards,
suddenly to arch –
the narrow back
a bone riddle –
and the plum-womb swang.

Then we made her a bed-box,
a home of moused
jerseys to nestle.
Into it
gladly she sagged,
all draping limbs,
all dropping paws,
all pregnant uterus,
heavy and struggling.

One by One
she pushed
and slid them blind out
into the
white air;
splurted them liquidly
from their
tough little sacks;
chewed through the
tiny slimey cords

that joined them
to her;
Rough tongued,
rasped them dry;
Nuzzled them to the
nipples in her
deep fur belly;
Gobbled hungrily
the afterbirth.

Ottilie Hainsworth

Calf

Little brown backed
square nosed calf,
funny head,
your curled forelock
between two
nub horns,
tripping
dainty with arrogance.

You have a
large, pale, gentle
nose and tongue
of wet velvet;
A milky, whiskery chin;
A pampered, childish, demanding
        "moo".

Star chested
baby bullock,
strident on
four sturdy legs,
They'll have you
hooked by one
dainty-smelly hoof,
heavily hung-swung,
wheeling and lumbering in terror.

They'll murder
    split
    stretch
    skin
    scoop gutless.

That swollen pink
gag of a tongue
    will be
    wrenched rootless;
That sweet breath of meadow
    a slaughtered
    blood still.

Ottilie Hainsworth

Earth Monster

The Earth Monster
crawled into our kitchen
yesterday morning;
Slunk belly-grovelling
rubbling and
gravelling.
I heard its
acorn-knuckledraffle
upon our table
where it sat,
its snake-black
trunk-thighs
splitted
moist
with whitish
close-clumps
of mushroom swollen
there.

Everyone stared at
the strange face of Earth,
the blushed clay jowls,
the roselips
slippery with fresh rain,
the frown of furred
rusted moss,
and behind glossy crocus lids
two pure
mulberry round eyes.

If you carved Earth
into halves
you'd find its organs.
A pulsing squash
of pure gold,
two jellied
naked lychees,
a pink, muscular guava,
and a heart
as tough skinned
as sweet-blooded
as beetroot.

When Moon was
pin-curled pretty
on night-time's silent shoulder,
Monster crept from our kitchen.
I think it will come again
one day,
to cuddle us
in those
shyly lustrous
silver-boughs.

Ottilie Hainsworth

When

When lamps moan low,
groaning in windbreath
you will find me.

When grass grows, blowing,
falling in sunagony
you will come.

When thoughts fly, crying
dying in moonwane,
I wait.

Birds sing in the trees,
housewalls echo the promise,
ivy clambers, rustling with bees.

The door is open.

I have gone.

Leaving

Sun breaks on dawn bed
fine feathered stream
from eastern cloud rim

White wraiths wither
shocked into earth
by first birdsong

You, rising from bed
startled by dawn kiss
mist into flight
before daylight
discovers our bond

Joy Hendry

Clearances

The wind sucks clouds. In the indrawn breath
grass bends and nods, like Mandarins.
The sun hunches, and begins to set no sooner
than it's risen. This
depopulated place ! Where moorland birds
repeat a sound, like copper, beaten.
The very moon imagines things –
a desert dusk, with itself as scimitar.
As the wind keeps up, closer than
I've heard my name in . . . how long?
and the dark coheres; an old idea
returns again, the prodigal friend:
of leaving: for Szachewan, or Persia.

Kathleen Jamie

49

Peter the Rock

The last trumpet of sunlight blows over the sea.
Pride. He moves high on the cliff
and raises and arm. The figures connect.
He pulls up and leans out, hair falling straight towards earth.

He tells me he dreams about nothing
but falling, though we sleep on the sand.
His arms always round me, golden hair
spilled over my face. That mysterious injury
torn in his shoulders: 'I told you, I fell.'

Even in kissing you feel for holds,
grip through to bone.
It doesn't surprise me, I do it myself,
enrage you with symbol, the meaning of things.
You practice moves and hate gestures,
God-talk with vengeance, imperfect shoulders.

I change the tapes. He drives, and will go on denying
into the night. There is nothing
but rock and the climbing of rock under the sun.
Which I say is falling and setting behind us, unfolded,
flashed in the wing mirrors, golden, your skin tone.

Kathleen Jamie

Sweat

A hinting and harking of marmite and fox,
musk and fritillaria;
a delicate something from the sea,
from the woods.
Real sweat trails memories
like comet tails of tiny stars
fizzing in the brain; sends signals
clear as morse,
naked as tongues;
bells boldy, through deoderant and talc,
a message from the armpit of the soul.

Sweat,
a sweet, sweet feather
tickling the fibres of the mind to song.

The mothers

The mothers move in pentacles of milky mystery
they are fountains and fruit bowls,
pomegranates riot on their robes.

The mothers whisper, envying my dream-filled nights
and pitying my childless, childish womb.
They see me getting away with it.

There is a carnal conspiracy, a sisterhood of stretch-marks,
its acolytes dance nightly in the teething rings,
blessed by the father's hand.

I merely recycle myself like the barren moon;
a modest metamorphosis, waxing and waning
in self-contained renaissance.

Paula Jennings

51

Daphne (a poem for two voices)

The child in a suburban bed
nests in soft branches,
sees a flower with a woman's face
that smiles and trills
a song she understands.

> *Daphne in the flowers*
> *picking more than she can give away,*
> *trying to encompass beauty in an afternoon*
> *gathering the four corners of a starry field*
> *into her lap.*

A tail of light on the rug,
the door shuts. There is darkness
and her father. There are hands
and a voice of fur:
don't tell, don't tell.

> *Daphne sees the man.*
> *He is eyes in a bush, wooden eyes with hands.*
> *Everything slows; the flowers falling slowly,*
> *the feet moving slowly,*
> *the shadow on the field.*

The child lies silent,
withdraws inside numb flesh.
Her father is the stranger in the park
(this is not happening)
his hands belong to someone else
(I am not here)
the frozen spirit chants
I am wood
I am wood.

leaves,
pounding, panic,
spurts of dust in the empty air.
The hands grab
(this is not happening)
the girl falls
(I am not here)
the spirit tears free
I am a tree
I am a tree.

Paula Jennings

In the Greek myth Daphne is pursued by Apollo who intends to rape her. She calls to her father, a river god, for help and he
changes her into a laurel tree.)

Married bliss

That night, she lay awake and listened to
the traffic going home past her window
and she listened to the clock
and she listened for a click in the lock
and listened to the neighbours talking through the wall
and listened for a footfall
and listened to her heart beat faster
and the meter in the hall clocked another unit
and she counted the units
and the heart beats
and the tick tocks
and every time she missed
she said – so this is married bliss.

Helen Lamb

Heatwave

Hot days and restless nights
the breeze won't come till our eyes are closed
sitting in the backyard – women talking
watering the seeds of mixed blessings.

They open up like flowers.
They are flowers
in marigold and fuschia cottons
letting down their straps
and rolling up their hair.
Their voices murmur amid the insect hum
meld with honey bees in the nasturtiums
and laughter sputters out across the lawn
as memories of men are mocked.
Placid men and brutal men
hungry men and randy men
men who must be apologised for
and men who must be praised.
The women turn sun-dazed onto their bellies
shrugging off children
who clamber and straddle their backs.

Hot days and reestless nights
the breeze won't come till our eyes are closed
women in the backyard – swatting flies
and singing lullabies to grubby, worn out kids.

Helen Lamb

Atlantic

who is there
to cross this sea with me?

grandmother, old in Donegal
looked at spray, day by day

red cliffs, white surf, green sea
Atlantic, hammering free

grandmother, convey me too
night crossings, solitude
you knew

small house on cliff's frown
America down, down
over horizon

you lived the line
between home and unknown

house and walled garden
cliffs and wild sea

who can match these antagonists?

I cannot cross alone

Mary McCann

English teacher

Miss Laird said
Lycidas
was the touchstone of English poetry

Miss Laird, brushing
her white lion hair
from her white powdered face

forever standing
at that battle scarred desk

her hands crusted with rings

lost her fiance in the war, we said

Miss Laird talked on
bewitched by Milton

while we sighed
and thought of rock'n'roll

weep no more, woeful shepherds
weep no more
said Miss Laird

for Lycidas your sorrow is not dead

her eyes shining like stars

when I consider how my light is spent
are half my days

moved to tears, melted
by a handful of words

she never finished Hamlet
in time for the Highers

Miss Laird was dilly dallying
in Act One

at sixteen we knew it all
oh, Miss Laird, we said
(throwing gym shoes across at the boys
and thinking of gold nail varnish
and paper taffeta petticoats)

she gets sent by Milton

old white lion
I hear her now

they also serve who only stand and wait

says Miss Laird

Mary McCann

57

responsible

my mouth is full of knives
and hammers and punches
which is why I do not open it too wide

but speak with care
through the smallest possible opening
filtering the words with my teeth

sometimes it is hard to be silent
with the bullets jumping around, and the flame-throwers
but my jaw is strong enough to keep control

do you realise what damage I could cause?
it's lucky for you people that I am responsible
I grind my teeth and choose my words with care.

Labyrinth

Robin is making a labyrinth in the garden
cutting an old question into the harmlesness of grass
with curved precision; Robin is a star,
is sharp and golden, and his pointed fingers
make a spiral imprint on the green.

in the evening, its edges collect darkness
and coils flex, lovely as muscle
Robin has let a snake into the garden,
a knowing creature, one of ideas
and of a certain arced direction;
night rises, and the house is lulled to sleep;
outside, the labyrinth flickers.

Ruth McIlroy

Heather markets

Huddled against the landrover
our German guests succumb
to the spoor of the glen.
The first sight is always impressive,
they arrive in thundering waves
a long established tribute
for the pibroch of the horn.

Before the sacks have burst
Grant sprints towards the slope
with the usual gruesome warning.
Exalted, the hunters capture
every neck-bending monarch.
Tonight the rafters will ring
with the warm vigour of manhood.

If one purple image
can linger in the brain, then
the whole elaborate charade
may survive another season.
Guests are a natural feature
we want them to return
as much as the hinds.

Maureen MacNaughton

Ghosts

You could have knocked me down
with a feather
when she said
that's never an oilrig
it's a neolithic stone structure
encircling
what's left of humanity.
So,
I looked again,
the sea sparkled
winked at my sunstruck sight
saying
don't trust just one sense.
Before
our horizons
the near haze
held ten platforms
landmarks
to the illusions of identity
reminders
of our almost history.

Annmarie MacRury

Catterline in winter

The wind gasps at the cliffs
And the sea roars and crashes
Through the conglomerate teeth
That defend the bay;
Fifteen feet of water and momentum
Edging the great round wound
Sucked by the backwash
With passionate care,
Sculpting stone patterns,
Seaweed edged.
On the beach,
Sea-dog views earth-dog from close
As the fishers' cottages
Cling on the cliff-top,
Their toes gripping the land,
Their rooves held on
Like hats.

Fevered and shivering,
I pick about the stones,
Hoping for the odd gate,
Wishing for an aspirin,
And finding only
Broken bottles
And nature's concrete.
The cormorants ride out
The weather, unsinkable, like corks,
And we look from the jetty
At grey-green growling water.
Above us,
Around a corner early in the morning,
The light shines its last
Until tonight
At Todhead.

In the house
At no.2
The stoves smoke,
According to the wind.
We cough and drink tea
And keep warm.
The earth-dog curls up
in front of the heat,
Toasting herself.
The sea-dog is out there,
In the weather.

Elektra's dance

I play on my ginger violin
A furious stamping dance,
A hot mixture
Of Bach and E major,
As kind of cure;
Pills to purge melancholy.
Each note rattles against the ceiling –
The children scream, burnt.
Who cares ? Not I –
Spicy springing fingertips on strings,
Sparks flying.
This kind of violence knows no bounds.
This is music to murder with –
Justifiably.

Susan Maťašovská

Word – soup

A waste of paper
Has a double meaning.
A double entendre
Does not, however, mean
That you heard it twice,
Or even thrice.
Remember the man
Who drank
Three cups of tea,
Three spoons of sugar in each
Blessed himself (+ + +) Amen
And cut his throat three times.
There is no simple reading
Of a set of facts.
Words are stronger
Than you would
Like them to be.
Get this stew,
This soup of particles
And participles
On the go,
And eat the dictionary.
It'll do you good.

Susan Maťašovská

Wedding

(for Ewan)

At the wedding
you came back to me
with other women's perfume
on your clothes, your hair.

They came
floating in chiffon
spike heels sinking
in the lawn:

Women
big with the absences
of children.

I knew you would impress;
less with your heavy head
inevitable on my breast,
than with the chance you gave
to flirt with their past lives
at husbands in grey suits
who turned back
to drinks and mantalk.

Oh I could have laughed,
mother to the trees and the sky and the grass,
if they had not, like great birds,
snatched you off;
fluttering up to the rest of the flock,
crooning and clucking:
Couldn't you just take him home?
Doesn't he put you in the notion?

At the wedding you came back
heavy with secrets;
your body curled to fit.

I will not know all
the perfume
of your days to come.

What I have is this:
in the quiet room
with the coats
I fed you and you smiled.

And the tree at the window
threw out its branches
and glittered its leaves
in such wild joy.

Downstairs
the wedding went on.

Alison Miller

A woman alone

A woman comforts a man, staring
Beyond his pillowed head, thinking
Of other things, of needful cooking and sewing,
Of flowers in a vase, or the idea of God.
She is giving only her body.
But the man is comforted, he does not know,
Blinded by customary eyes, lips, breasts, tender hands,
That the woman's mind is faithless.
It is not with him,
Nor with any man, for to her all men are children.
She has been sucked by baby men, freely giving her body
As she now gives it.
Suckling, she thought of other things,
Staring out gently over over small, breast-pillowed heads, thinking.
Faithless.
The woman alone.

Naomi Mitchison

The hunchback in the cellar

The hunchback in the cellar
admits no-one but me
I bear a sheaf of ancient papers
their tattered folds too brittle
ever to smooth again
and drifted soot obscures
the marks I sensed in darkness
my fingers smutted with secrecy
but Quasimodo winks and nods
towards the humming red machine
the rotted cord
breaks with a touch
I trust the magic engine
which charges dust and fixes shadow
to reproduce the hidden images
black spiders' ghosts
against the crisp white sheets.

unreachable

fist over starving fist
I climb
the braided rope
that issues from my belly
where the greedy navel mouth
devours hungry
every inch I gain
and over me still hangs
unreachable
the vast white moon

Joy Pitman

full circle

I have passed to the centre
of the maze
gone round full circle
and emerged again

I was not lost

I saw you to the door and said goodnight
put out the light
and turned to face the rising day

and if you say I cried upon your shoulder
– it was at old betrayals
for you have not diminished me

I have gone under
held my breath
surfaced
and breathed again

I did not drown

Joy Pitman

Second threshold

Jist lay yer haans in mine
And naething say,
Though fegs it's mony a spate
that's gushed
Sin yon ill day
Fin you and me
Broke tryst
And took oor sep'rate way.

Sae muckle tae explain ! –
Routh o life's storms
Throu years we sinnert spent
In fremmit airms –
Aa by;
And noo we've met,
Nae menseless wastefu wishin
Nae regret –
Jist tak my haans in yours;
Wi benediction lay
Yer urgent mou on mine
And naething say.

Lilianne Grant Rich

A woman's muse

1
Even midsummer's honeyed joys
are not enough
for me, married to the inmost Breath
men call the Muse.

Have I espoused my animus,
a god deep-chested with fire and thrust?
Or is it indeed a woman I have loved,
my fertile darling, ripe as hidden fruit,
hedged with thorns ?

I pick with an addict's haste
and tear my outstretched arms,
never sated or replete
until, wedded to the one I dare not woo
I bring forth words.

2
No great daimon possesses me;
    no goddess visits here,
but in the rustling fields at harvest time
    beneath a mellow sun
      a woman gleans
    the tossing wheat, the fronded bere.
Her sickle scythes the words I rhyme.

My poems ripen in this woman's dream
    and I am drawn to the gleam
      of her hearth-fire;
    its heat too obsolete and mean
      to forge
    the weaponry of war and power
with which the world is lost and won:
but at this flame my song is spun.

Jenny Robertson

Chambered cairn

1   The skulls

Skulls look heavy as weathered stones,
polished by tides, cast high on the shore,
but weigh as little, are as brittle
as seagull eggs.

2   The girl

Her teeth gleam, firmly bedded into bone.
The brain has gone
and, with those soft cells, her identity.

From infancy she bore loads
whose drag and pull
moulded her soft skull.
she carried boulders for her men
to hammer into tombs.

Was she just a drudge, a slave,
tossed in orgy, incest, lust,
worn out at twenty-six and cast
into the chambered grave?
Or did she smile, dance, feast,
crunch hazelnuts, thread beads?

Her tale's untold.
Only her indented skull
with malformed fontanelle
maps the contours of her toil.

3   The hammer

A boy found an oblong stone
among the boulders in the bay.
He pondered over it, tried it, weighed it
in his right hand
and took it home.

There he moulded it, making a grip
for fingers and thumb,
polished it and banged it,
building walls to keep out
wind and tide.

He could not know that his hammer
would be uncovered by a plough,
and, like a signpost, point the way
to his people's burial place
beside the rocky bay.

He could not know that the walls he made
would be evidence
of a life and culture here
older than pyramids.

4   The pot

A woman tossed her tangled hair
from her low forehead streaked with clay
and pressed her fingernails
deeper in designs she made
around a soft, new-moulded jar.

The wind from the sea
brought her patterns of waves on stones.

She heard seals sing,
saw a sea eagle circling in,
and knew her pot would be a lucky one.

"This will do me and my bairns,
Maybe my grandchildren will press
their soft, sharp nails
into these marks when I am dead and gone."

Children press curious nails in the marks she made,
feel the shape of fifty centuries;
from higher foreheads toss back windswept hair
and call to seals swimming in the bay.

5   Bead and eagles' claws

In jet and molar, limpet shell and bone
tribesmen bore holes
to thead their necklaces
on thongs, and thrust
over strong knuckles smoothed, official rings.

Scattered among broken pots and bones
these tokens outlasted love and rank.

But some bones lay unequally
in niches in the high curved tomb.
The tally of eagles' claws
attested status: chieftain,
princeling or warrior priest,
whose robes and ritual are lost,
and, mute as stones, their songs.

Jenny Robertson

Fertility doll

I'm nearly done – the belly
like a hand thrown bowl swells
with a homespun lack of symmetry
I swerve off-plumb.
I'm warm brown, a baked-clay shade
glazed to the sheen
of egg-brushed bread. A wholesome loaf
proving in the sun.

My days are numbered. All the same
my indolence is huge, my balance
precarious. This taut bulk
threatens to topple.

The man who made me cut me short
lopped off my legs, stuck
to the stumps two tiny feet –
his last caprice before dusk.

I was a laborious task. Now
my crammed mass is stilted,
pegged to the earth's crust –
expecting dawn.

Dilys Rose

No name woman

All day she feeds the drunken menfolk
on the terrace. Between meals they gamble,
quarrrel and groom their fighting cocks.
With one eye on her youngest child
(grubbing in the dirt for bugs)
she stirs the rice, ladles broth
from spoon to bowl, fans back
the ubiquitous flies. Steaming pots
and hot fat spit their hiss at her.
She wears the same rags constantly
a hand-me-down print wrap, the patttern
washed away, the hem a tatter –
eats her dinner standing up
then clears and lays more tables
cradling plates to hush their clatter.
When only the rats nag for more
she sweeps the dirt floor clean.

Dilys Rose

Lois of the garden

Lois of the garden
greenhouse, summer garden,
picking up the plastic toys,
half broken,
strewn around the garden.
Lois of the very busy
"not doing much"
but managing.

House of the half-baked cake.
Through lounge.
Lois of the crazy
paving garden path
half open gate.
I half remember her
half-made glove puppets,
lifeless dreams,
dead on the kitchen table.
Lois of the water hose
out in the sunbaked garden.
I half remembered her.

Then suddenly I saw her
life of the stage
makeshift, shift over now,
light-footed, sleight of hand,
stage light, upstage,
out front.
Stage in amongst us,
dancing and singing
and bringing us in.
Lois of the tambourine,
Lois of the one day now,
Lois of the "I will somehow".

Then I knew her,
Lois of the fol-de-rol,
Lois of the interval,
the wide-eyed smile,
the lemonade,
the change of scene,
harlequinade, the drum
the tambourine,
the twirling skirt, the wonderland,
the goose that laid . . .
the Lois of the outstretched hand.

Wendy de Rusett

The gap

They take out what is dead inside.
This happens.
The white coat says, 'I'm sorry.'
It is not a day of decisions then.
They operate.

The day before I had wondered
at the wind and rain swayed trees
trees out of the centre of town
trees not in the country
long worn-out arms going
backwards and forwards not pin-
pointing, on a darkening night, wettening.

A hole to go into not understanding
profound as on one night a heartbeat
the next night none.
At first, two small humans,
a clutch of hearts on the hospital drive
and inside one, a derangement of the senses,
pushed pulled unchoosing
her blood as yet unexposed
not sloshed over the gap

bed bed bed beds
clean sheeted happenings
an awful eyefull of women
Slowly up the ward comes
the distended stomach of a lack of womb.
She smiles
and then I cramped and
found hills and dips of pain and relief
and lost the good safe clock.
what? what is coming out?

Next day, the white coat
from its scan, its map
said there was certainty.
This was not a day of decisions then
as all the days before had been –
abortion or a mummy?
What dies when someone else is born?
This was a day for an operation.
They evacuate the womb

but afterwards at home
the monstrous cow rushed out of the womb,
wrong, bellowing her terror!
A dream. I got up. Then I met
in the bathroom, staring at me,
an animal, an abortion,
the silken survival of a cat that
howled and fled as I screamed.

Maureen Sangster

The Owners' child

The Owners' child
appears in pink
at the party
in the church hall.

The Owners' child
dazzles in lemon
at the family reunion
in the hotel.

The Owners' child
turns up in orange
in the backseat
on holiday
in the Borders.

The Owners' child
wants to
puke in green over every
colour in the Owners' world.

Maureen Sangster

Deep-water terminal

You like names like that, you said,
The day we went to the James river,
Drove along the Old Gun Road,
Sun hot and heavy,
Trees coloured like a child's paint-box.
I stepped in the mud,
And it oozed between my toes,
So I waded in the river, to clean them.
Big steamers come miles up the river, you said,
As far as deep-water terminal.

We went to Babe's restaurant, before I left,
To drink some wine.
The waitress hugged two men at the next table,
She almost skipped across the floor,
Her eyes were blue and bright.
She put candles on all the tables.
It was getting dark, and we were talking
About dreams, supernatural things,
And inexplicable connexions between people.
You said you didn't believe in 'all that' anyway,
And your face was jumping in light and shadow.

You look to the side of people, when you talk,
You rarely catch their eyes.
Hidden by so many jokes and stories,
I imagine voyages in all your dreams,
Circling within the limits of your laughter.
I never dared to step within your boundaries
Although I thought I heard you calling
As if you thought that I was far away.

Morelle Smith

Highland

Snow on the high mountains
Is smoothed by the wind.
The white folds of winter
Fray into yellow grass
And sleeping heather.

There is no tree between me and the mountain.
Only the wind combing the marsh grass.

A ledge of snow forms a step to the house
And the sunlight trips, on its way to the ground.

Ballachulish in evening

Ballachulish in evening
Slips out of the water
Turning its back to the mountain behind.
Sunlight huddles
On the nether side of the hill
Like a myth from another land
Meaning held in its hand
Like a signpost the frost
And the wind have obscured
And Time has layered
With its restless sleep.
Ballachulish in evening
Slumbers
Downwind of Time.

Morelle Smith

Unconnected verses of war

If we pull the string
　　　the puppet will move
　　　　　　dance, dance.

Move over
give her a look at the sun
before they sweep her shavings from the floor.

They've got me lying face down
watching the man
who could be my father
smoking cigarettes
I remember a game called Green Lady
this is not it
I'm no longer young
the grass has been trodden out since then

If I kiss you
will you dance?

and she danced
and she cried for dancing

Maybe it will change
Maybe it will change for the better.

Put boots on to dance she said
the red mud will stain your ankles.

Karen Thomson

Paranoia

Do not try any harder for my benefit
your road to heaven is well lit
I'm falling behind, a fate put down to
my own doing,
Talk amongst yourselves whilst I leave the
room
Dare I ask why everyone else has a white
carnation and not me?
The band plays the wedding march
too loud an' I think someone has
stolen my shoe.
She said that you all sat up to
learn your lines in order to giggle
at my blankness
She also said that you're a long
time dead
Bet you all know what she means?

Karen Thomson

If I were a dog

She has come back from the dead,
she, whom they took away
at peace and ready for death.

Our grief is unspent
our funeral thwarted
as, unwanted, we welcome her home.
We, too, had tasted freedom.

Dressed and fed
she re-lives alone in the living room
sitting in grudged sunlight.
She is too good
or too bad for homes.

We crush her with news
of her cataracts.
She wishes she were dead.
"If I were a dog
I would have been put down."

She drops the cake plate
into the potato basket;
earth on the cake,
fear in her eyes.
She is inconsolable.

Slight and frail
she creeps to communion
helped gently all the way
up the long slow aisle.

Valerie Thornton

Silk moth ghosts

I slip silk on next to my skin.
I used to assume the exotic allusions too.

Yesterday I met the artisans
in a small glass box, in a glasshouse
in the rain.

Milk-pale, furry silk moths
with ragged wings outspread
crawled fluttering on the glass floor.

Benign and plump, unable to eat or fly,
the soft creamy creatures lay three days of eggs.

In a corner, spread-eagled,
a crumpled silk moth.

In another corner, a few limp mulberrry leaves,
for greedy green caterpillars preparing to spin
their thousand yards of finest pure silk
like a finger bandage around themselves.

Against the glass wall held by guys of silken thread,
a cocoon with dark fluid seeping out,
ruining the silk.

For my sensual silks, they unspin the cocoons
hundreds of times over.
What do they do with all the half-moths ?

I still slip on the sad soft silks
(shantung, tussore, crepe de chine)
and wonder where the gentle silk moth ghosts
are shivering.

Valerie Thornton

Biographical notes

Kate Armstrong, born 1944; teaches primary school and adult creative writers in Dundee; writes poetry and prose in English and Scots; translates from French and German; currently working on George Sand; personist rather than feminist; likes poetry read aloud.

Sheena Blackhall, born 1947, has had four collections of poems published, and a collection of her short stories (Scots) was launched in January 1989. Separated from her husband, she and her children live on Income Support.

Meg Bateman, was born in Edinburgh in 1959. She learnt Gaelic, which she now teaches, at Aberdeen University and in South Uist. Her poetry has been published in *Gairm* and *Chapman*, and a bilingual Gaelic/Irish collection is in preparation.

Rosalind Brackenbury is the author of eight novels and a book of poetry, *Telling Each Other It Is Possible*. She lives in Edinburgh where she teaches creative writing in the university's extra-mural department.

Sarah Busbridge was born in Surrey in 1963 and studied music at Huddersfield and Edinburgh, where she is currently doing a Phd on semiotics of song. She has written poetry intermittently for ten years.

Chris Cherry Writing poetry, living in Scotland, being active in education, promoting and pursuing opportunities for personal and professional development, are all important aspects of my life. I've written poetry since 1977, including *Dreaming Wild Honey*, a poem-play for four female voices.

Maggie Christie is in Pomegranate women's writing group. She makes a living indexing and copy-editing. A radical feminist, she helps produce *Edinburgh Women's Liberation Newsletter*, writes and plays music, researches women composers. She recently retired from toothfairyship, but santahood is harder to throw off.

Barbara Clarke was born in 1960, and lives in Edinburgh. She is a nurse, and a spinner, weaver and knitter. She is currently working on a novel.

Dot Clarke I come from Ayrshire. I lived in the country there for most of my first eighteen years. Then I studied history in Glasgow and Canada, worked in England and returned to Scotland, to Edinburgh, in 1982. The East is different from the West!

Helen Dunwoodie was born in Edinburgh in 1941, and has recently returned to live in the city with her two daughters. She is a student at Edinburgh University's Religious Studies Unit.

Margaret Elphinstone lives in Galloway, and has published a variety of poems and short stories. Her first novel, *The Incomer*, was published by The Women's Press in 1987. She is also the author of two gardening books, *The Holistic Gardener* (Thorsons 1987), and *Organic Gardening* (Greenprint 1989).

Sally Evans runs a cut-price bookstall on the corner of Lothian and Kings Stables Road in Edinburgh, and finds time to write during the bad weather.

Gerrie Fellows is an expatriate New Zealander with two passports and an English accent. Her poetry has appeared in *Edinburgh Review, Cencrastus, Writing Women*, and *Variant*, and has been recorded for STV's *In Verse* series. She lives in Glasgow.

Carol Galbraith Born 1930, Campbeltown, of seafaring and fishing people. Graduate of Glasgow University and winner of its McCash prize for Scots poetry. Singer (Mod gold medallist) and mathematics teacher. Married to Derick Thomson with one daughter and five sons.

Magi Gibson Born Kilsyth, 1953. Married with three young children. When time allows works as a tutor with the Workers' Educational Association.

Valerie Gillies Born Canada, 1948, lived as a child in the Southern Uplands of Scotland. Universities of Mysore, South India, and Edinburgh. Married to Professor William Gillies: three children. Currently Writer in Residence, Duncan of Jordanstone College of Art, Dundee.

Mary Gladstone writes. She is also an embroiderer, a gardener and a person who reads. She is a Scot. She lives in Edinburgh and survives there by writing and broadcasting for newspapers and the radio.

Thelma Good so dreads writing biographical notes that she rarely submits her work for publication and reads her poems to audiences instead. She lives on the edge of Edinburgh, in a village called Juniper Green, with a husband and two children.

Ottilie Hainsworth I was born in Edinburgh in 1969. I went to Stockbridge Primary and Drummond High School. In 1987 I was highly commended in the *Observer* National Children's Poetry Competition. I'm a student in first year at Glasgow School of Art.

Joy Hendry Born Perth 1953. Graduate in Mental Philosophy from University of Edinburgh. Dip.Ed. Taught English at Knox Academy for seven years. Editor of *Chapman* since 1972. Since 1984 freelance writer, editor and broadcaster. Edited (with Raymond Ross) *Sorley Maclean: Critical Essays* (Scottish Academic Press, 1986). Involved in campaign to create a National Theatre in Scotland, and in the committee which produced *A Claim of Right for Scotland* (CSA, 1988). Married. Lives in Edinburgh.

Kathleen Jamie was born in 1962. A graduate in philosophy, she has made a living as an archaeological "digger" and a pizza waitress. Her three books of poetry have brought her several awards. Now she is trying her hand at fiction.

Paula Jennings I was born in England in 1950 and have lived in Scotland for most of the past nineteen years. One of my main preoccupations is how to earn a living and still retain my vitality as a creative lesbian feminist. The search continues!

Helen Lamb, born in 1956, has had short stories in *Original Prints II* and on Radio 4's *Morning Story*. Studied at Glasgow University and now lives in Dunblane with her three children.

Mary McCann I was born during World War II, grew up in a small town in Ayrshire and now live in Edinburgh. I started writing when I became unemployed and have been in a women's writing group for about nine years.

Ruth McIlroy was born in 1956 in Wales, one of five sisters. She spent her early childhood in Jamaica, and was educated in Edinburgh, where she now lives. She has been involved in women's writing groups for several years.

Maureen MacNaughton is a Glaswegian now living in Aberdeen. Has been published in a variety of journals and anthologies, including *Voices* (Israel), *Poetry Review, New Coin* (South Africa), *Chapman*, and *Interstate* (USA).

Annmarie MacRury was born in 1962. Lives in Edinburgh and is Treasurer of the Edinburgh Writers Association who organise First Friday Poems and Pints, every month in the West End Hotel. Writes mainly poems and short stories. Likes interesting performance of current writing in relaxed settings.

Susan Maťašovskà now lives in Scotland after working abroad for some years. Originally a musicologist, she now writes prose, poetry (German and English), music criticism and essays, and teaches the violin for a living. She lives alone with her daughter.

Alison Miller Born in Orkney in 1952. I've lived in Glasgow for the last nine years. I work in Castlemilk for the Workers' Educational Association, running writers' workshops and other classes. I write when I can make the time.

Naomi Mitchison I started writing verse when I was ten and was delighted to be published in the school magazine. A little later Andrew Lang – who preferred his (un-successful) poems to his (successful) fairy tales – encouraged me to write verse and occasionally to win competitions. However, I did not write any good poems until I was around thirty. I went on writing after that, for some fifty years – some good poems, some bad – and that is more than enough time for anyone.

Joy Pitman was born in Bristol in 1945, moved to Scotland in 1973, has worked as a teacher, archivist, mother, publisher and administrator, and is currently training in psychotherapy. Her poems are published by Stramullion, Polygon and several Scottish magazines.

Lilianne Grant Rich Born Glenlivet, 1909, brought up on Speyside. Taught in Kirtlebridge, Dumfriesshire and Aberdeen. Married 1934, thereafter furth of Scotland for over thirty years. After being widowed returned to Scotland, and with intermittent worldwide travel has been 'based' in Aberdeen for twenty years. She has published four books of poetry in both Scots and English.

Jenny Robertson, a children's author, has published poems in magazines. A collection, *Beyond the Border*, is in preparation. Jenny teaches writing classes and lives and works with words to pattern a meaning, make a link, a celebration, a song.

Dilys Rose was born in Glasgow and now lives, mostly, in Edinburgh. A collection of poems (*Chapman*) and short stories (Secker and Warburg) are due to be published in autumn 1989.

Wendy de Rusett Born in Aberdeen, reared in Yorkshire. BA Philosophy (London). Worked in community relations, later taught art in Leeds. Member of a women artists' co-operative for seven years. Moved to Glasgow 1986. Freelance artist, enjoys hillwalking, traditional music and song.

Maureen Sangster Born Aberdeen, 1954. Now lives in Edinburgh. Began writing in 1981. Former member of Pomegranate Women's Writing Group. Her poetry has been published in magazines and in the collection *Different People* (Straight Line Publications). Currently unemployed.

Morelle Smith I have had poems and stories published in various magazines and anthologies in Scotland, England and Ireland, and am at present working on some longer pieces of prose.

Karen Thomson I'm 27, happily single with two vibrant daughters. My children, my class, my politics are my ability to fight on. Defeat is a luxury working class women cannot afford. We have survived. We will continue to survive with pride.

Valerie Thornton Born 1954 in Glasgow. Educated in Stirling and at Glasgow University. Former English teacher, now concentrating on writing, interspersed with work on feature films, film festivals and picture research. Has published poems and short stories in various outlets, including *Lines Review, Cencrastus, New Writing Scotland* and *Scottish Short Stories*.